Counting Books

Footballs
and
Falling Leaves

A Fall Counting Book

by Rebecca Fjelland Davis

Reading Consultant: Jennifer Norford
Senior Consultant: Mid-continent for Research and Education

Capstone
press

Mankato, MN

A+ Books are published by Capstone Press,
151 Good Counsel Drive, P.O. Box 669, Mankato, Minnesota 56002.
www.capstonepress.com

1 2 3 4 5 6 11 10 09 08 07 06

Library of Congress Cataloging-in-Publication Data
Davis, Rebecca Fjelland.
    Footballs and falling leaves: a fall counting book / by Rebecca Fjelland Davis.
    p. cm.—(A+ books. Counting books)
    Includes bibliographical references and index.
    ISBN-13: 978-0-7368-5376-7 (hardcover)
    ISBN-10: 0-7368-5376-6 (hardcover)
    1. Counting—Juvenile literature. 2. Autumn—Juvenile literature. I.
Title. II. Series.
QA113.D38 2006
513.2'11—dc22
                                            2005019036

Credits
Jenny Marks, editor; Ted Williams, designer; Karon Dubke, photographer; Kelly Garvin, photo
    researcher

Photo Credits
Capstone Press, Karon Dubke, cover (bus, footballs, pumpkins), 2–3 (all), 4–5, 10–11 (all),
    12–13 (all), 16–17 (all), 26–27 (buses), 28
Corbis/Ariel Skelley, 24–25; Patrick Johns, 18–19; W. Wayne Lockwood, 9; Yva Momatiuk, 6–7
Creatas, 22–23 (all), 26–27 (geese)
Photodisc, cover (acorn), 14–15 (all), 20–21 (all), 26 (leaves), 27 (acorns), 29 (all)

Note to Parents, Teachers, and Librarians
Footballs and Falling Leaves uses color photographs and a rhyming nonfiction format to introduce
children to various signs of the fall season while building mastery of basic counting skills. It is
designed to be read aloud to a pre-reader or to be read independently by an early reader. The images
help early readers and listeners understand the text and concepts discussed. The book encourages
further learning by the following sections: Facts about Fall, Words to Know, Read More, Internet
Sites, and Index. Early readers may need assistance using these features.

Summer is over, winter draws near.

The season called fall is finally here.

Leaves turn colors in cooler weather.

Let's find fall things to count together.

3

1

One brown football, hear the crowd cheer. Football season means that fall is really here.

Two furry bears fatten up in fall. They will sleep all winter and they won't eat at all.

Three farm combines moving
oh so slow. They cut golden
grain row after row.

9

Four yellow buses roll down the street. Heading back to school— quick, grab a seat!

5

Five orange pumpkins
for Halloween night.
Five scary jack o' lanterns
will be quite a sight.

6

Six brown acorns,
PLOP! PLOP! they fall.
Watch the busy squirrels
burying them all.

7

Seven ears of corn,
just what farmers need
to store for the winter
as animal feed.

Eight red apples, my oh
my. Won't they taste good,
baked in a pie?

9

Nine colored leaves
gently float down.
Red, orange, and brown
cover the ground.

Ten plump geese fly through
the sky. HONK! HONK! HONK!
They sound their goodbye.

10

23

Darkness comes sooner day after day.

School and football. Chores and play.

There are so many things to do in fall.

It's hard to find time to finish them all.

How Many?

Leaves

Buses

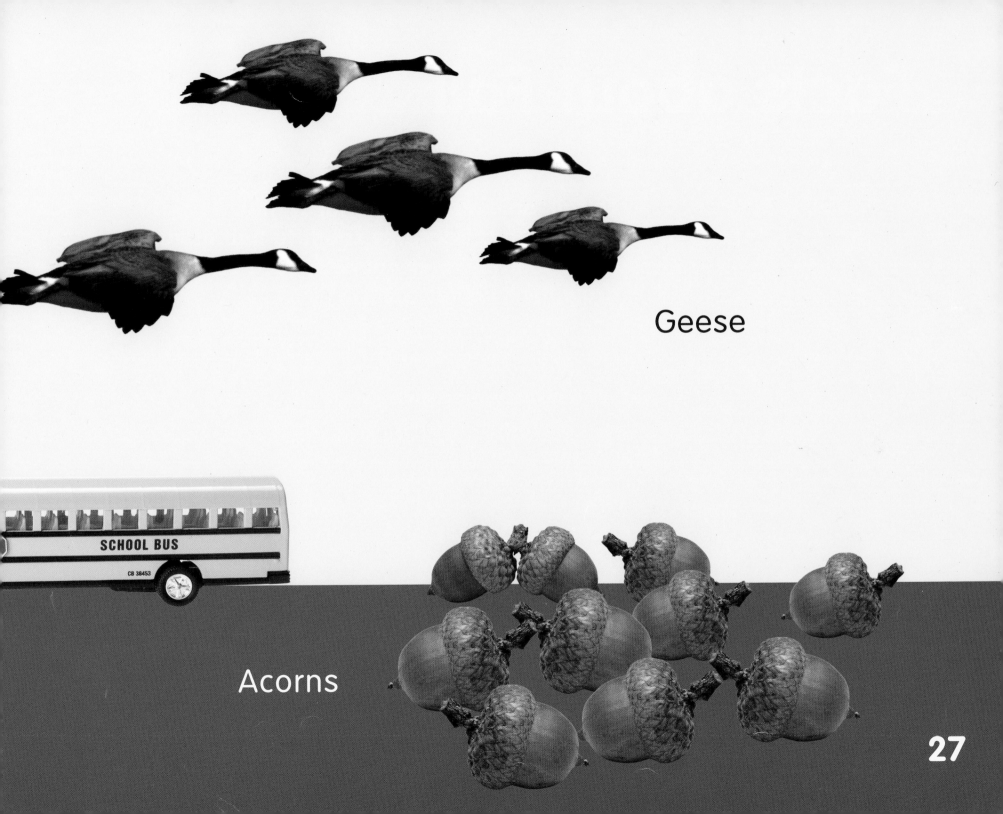

Geese

SCHOOL BUS
CB 38453

Acorns

Facts about Fall

In fall, animals prepare for winter. Squirrels gather food. Geese fly south to find a warm place to live. Other animals, such as bears, grow thick winter coats.

Not all black bears have black fur. Their fur can be black, brown, blonde, or even white.

Squirrels aren't the only ones who eat acorns. Long ago, people ground acorns into flour and made acorn pancakes.

People use machines to pick most crops, but apples must be picked by hand.

Leaves change colors because some types of trees stop making food in the fall. Water stops flowing to the leaves. The leaves dry up and turn yellow, orange, red, and brown.

When Canada geese and other birds fly south for winter, it is called migrating.

Words to Know

acorn (AY-korn)—the nut of an oak tree; an oak seed is inside an acorn.

combine (KAHM-bine)—a big farm machine used to harvest grain and other crops

grain (GRAYN)—the seed of a cereal plant, such as corn, oats, and wheat

jack o' lantern (JACK OH LAN-turn)—a pumpkin with a face carved into it

migrate (MYE-grate)—to move from one area to another; many birds migrate in fall to find warmer areas to live during the winter.

season (SEE-zuhn)—one of the four parts of the year; autumn, winter, spring, and summer are seasons.

weather (WETH-ur)—the conditions outside

Read More

Maurer, Tracy Nelson. *A to Z of Autumn.*
A to Z. Vero Beach, Fla.: Rourke, 2003.

Parker, Victoria. *Fall.* Raintree Sprouts.
Chicago: Heinemann, 2005.

Schlepp, Tammy J. *Seasons.* My World.
Brookfield, Conn.: Copper Beech Books, 2000.

Whitehouse, Patricia. *Seasons ABC.* Chicago:
Heinemann, 2003.

Internet Sites

FactHound offers a safe, fun way to find Internet sites related to this book. All of the sites on FactHound have been researched by our staff.

Here's how:
1) Visit *www.facthound.com*
2) Type in this special code **0736853766** for age-appropriate sites. Or enter a search word related to this book for a more general search.
3) Click on the "**FETCH IT**" button.

FactHound will fetch the best sites for you!

Index